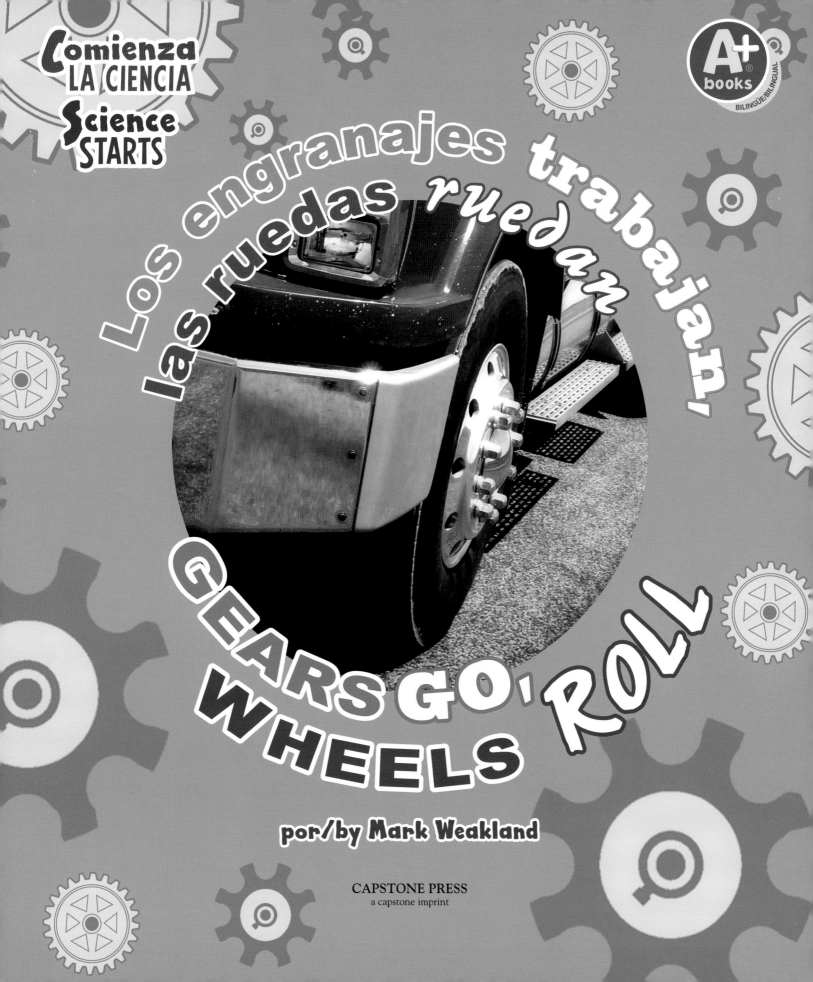

Comienza
LA CIENCIA
Science
STARTS

A+
books
BILINGÜE/BILINGUAL

Los engranajes trabajan,
las ruedas ruedan

GEARS GO,
WHEELS ROLL

por/by Mark Weakland

CAPSTONE PRESS
a capstone imprint

Wheels are all around us. At the fair a Ferris wheel spins gracefully in the night. While unseen wheels turn inside clocks and computers, most others are easy to spot.

Las ruedas están en todo nuestro alrededor.
En la feria la noria gira con elegancia en la noche.
Mientras ruedas que no vemos giran dentro de relojes
y computadoras, muchas otras son fáciles de ver.

Wheels come in all sizes. Small wheels roll under rollerblades, scooters, and skateboards.

Hay ruedas de todos los tamaños. Las ruedas pequeñas ruedan debajo de patines, monopatines y patinetas.

Buses, race cars, and
semitrucks rumble along
on big wheels.

Los autobuses, autos de
carrera y camiones ruedan
sobre ruedas grandes.

Tractors roll through fields on big and small wheels. Tractor tires fit perfectly between rows of crops so plants won't get crushed.

Los tractores ruedan por los campos sobre ruedas pequeñas y grandes. Las ruedas del tractor encajan perfectamente entre hileras de cultivos para que las plantas no se aplasten.

No matter the size, wheels make it easy to move people and objects.

Sin importar el tamaño, las ruedan facilitan mover gente y objetos.

Without wheels you would have to drag
that wagon or carry heavy weights.
Why work so hard?

Sin ruedas tendrías que arrastrar
el carrito o cargar cosas pesadas.
¿Por qué trabajar tan duro?

We use wheels to travel quickly and easily. Buses, cabs, subways, and trains use wheels. Airplanes use them when leaving and landing.

Nosotros usamos ruedas para viajar rápida y fácilmente. Autobuses, taxis, subterráneos y trenes usan ruedas. Los aviones las usan cuando despegan y aterrizan.

Tricycles cruise on three wheels.
Motorcycles zoom away on
two. Can you think of
something with just
one wheel?

Los triciclos andan
en tres ruedas.
Las motocicletas
pasan volando en dos.
¿Puedes pensar en algo
que tenga una sola rueda?

11

On a wheelbarrow, one wheel turns around one axle.

En una carretilla, una rueda gira alrededor de un eje.

axle/eje

Axles hold wheels in place while allowing them to turn. For wheels to work, they need an axle.

Los ejes sostienen a las ruedas en su lugar al mismo tiempo que permiten que giren. Para que las ruedas funcionen, necesitan un eje.

Doorknobs act like two wheels. Connected by an axle in the door, turning a doorknob moves the latch.

Los picaportes actúan como dos ruedas. Conectados por un eje en la puerta, cuando giramos un picaporte se mueve el pestillo.

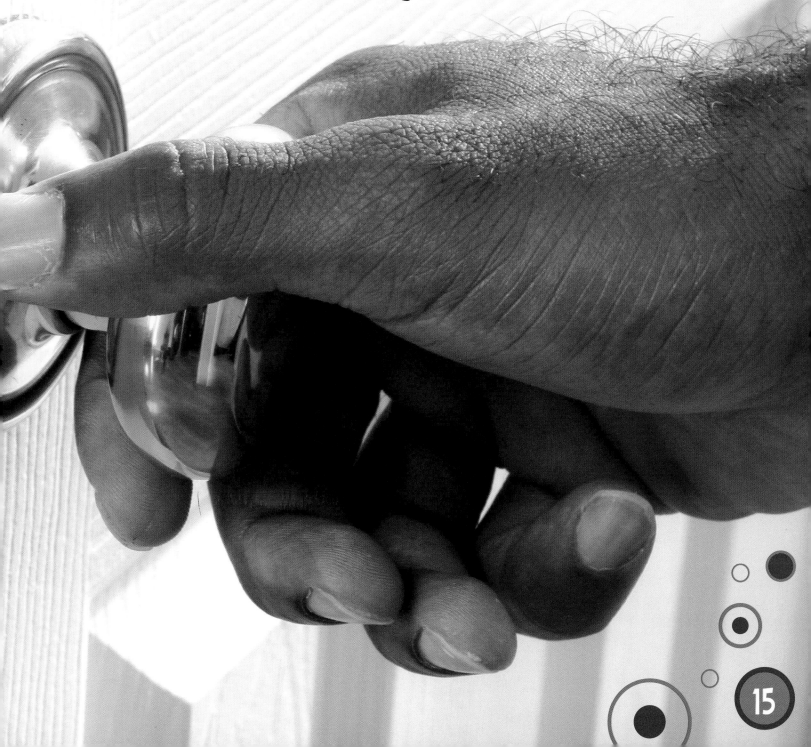

Turn the knob, and you're
turning a wheel!

Gira el picaporte y ¡estás
girando una rueda!

15

There are many wheels and axles on a car.

Hay muchas ruedas y ejes en un automóvil.

Two front wheels turn around one axle. Two back wheels use another.

Dos ruedas frontales giran alrededor de un eje. Dos ruedas traseras usan otro.

pulley/
polea

A pulley is a type of wheel.
Pull on the rope, and the
sail rushes to the top of the
ship's mast.

Una polea es un tipo de rueda.
Tira de la cuerda y la vela
sube rápidamente hacia lo
más alto en el mástil
del barco.

On a crane many pulleys work together. With pulleys and cables, a crane can lift lots of metal.

En una grúa muchas poleas trabajan juntas. Con las poleas y los cables, una grúa puede levantar muchos metales.

19

Gears are special kinds of wheels. Every gear
is ringed with teeth. The teeth fit together,
so one gear can turn many others.
Can you see the teeth?

Los engranajes son tipos especiales de ruedas.
Cada engranaje tiene dientes a su alrededor.
Los dientes encajan entre sí, de manera que
un engranaje puede hacer girar a muchos
otros. ¿Puedes ver los dientes?

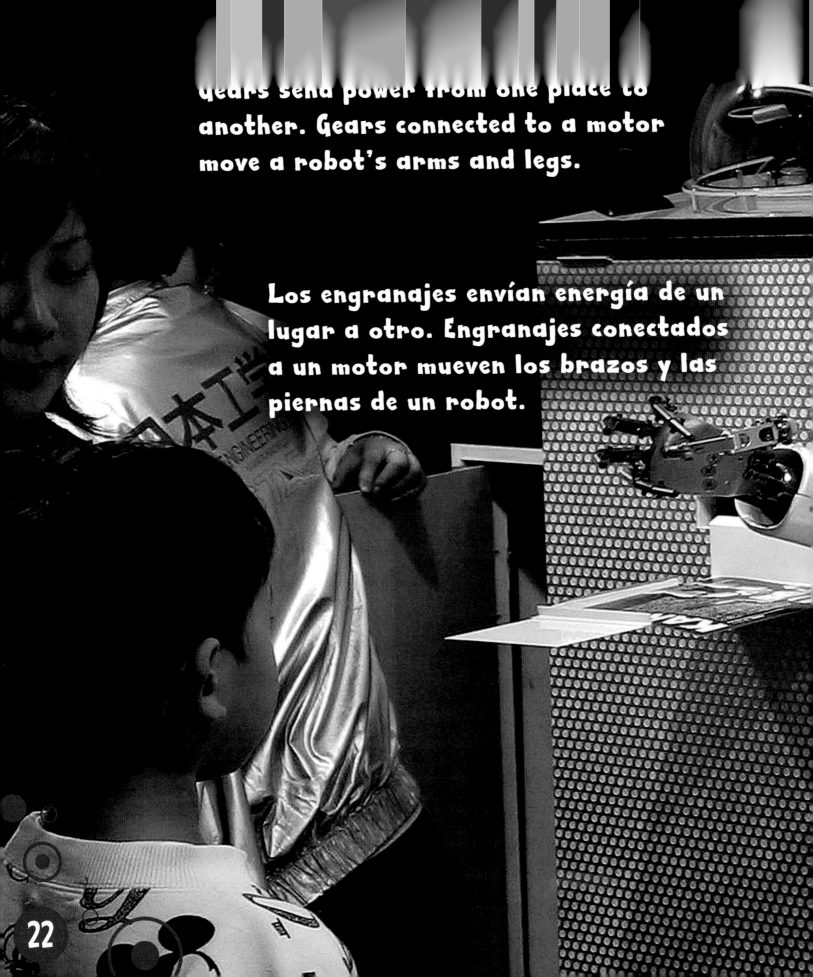

Gears send power from one place to another. Gears connected to a motor move a robot's arms and legs.

Los engranajes envían energía de un lugar a otro. Engranajes conectados a un motor mueven los brazos y las piernas de un robot.

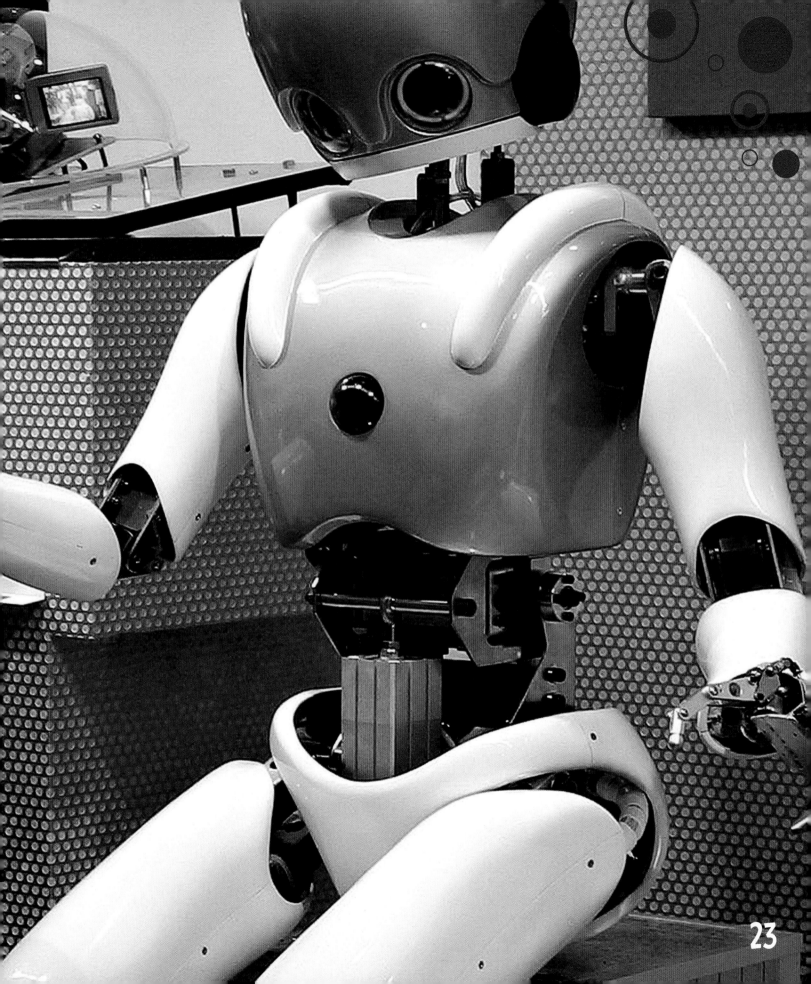

Bicycles have gears with large teeth. The front gears are linked to the back gears by a bike chain.

Las bicicletas tienen engranajes con dientes grandes. Los engranajes del frente están ligados a los engranajes de atrás por una cadena de bicicleta.

Gears, a chain, and strong legs power a bike's back wheel.

Los engranajes, una cadena y piernas fuertes hacen funcionar la rueda trasera de la bicicleta.

Watches and clocks with hands contain many gears. Tiny gears quietly whirr and buzz, spinning round and round. The gears turn the second hand, minute hand, and hour hand.

Los relojes de pulsera y los relojes con manecillas tienen muchos engranajes. Engranajes diminutos runrunean y zumban, dando vueltas una y otra vez. Los engranajes hacen girar la manecilla de los segundos, la manecilla de los minutos y la manecilla de la hora.

27

Wheels and gears are busy doing
work all around us.

Las ruedas y los engranajes están ocupados
realizando tareas a todo nuestro alrededor.

Slowly churning the water, a paddle wheel pushes a boat up a river. What other wheels and gears have you seen?

Agitando las aguas lentamente, una rueda de paletas empuja el bote en el río. ¿Qué otras ruedas y engranajes has visto?

Glossary

axle—a bar in the center of a wheel around which a wheel turns

cable—a thick wire

crane—a machine with a long arm used to lift and move heavy objects

gear—a toothed wheel that fits into another toothed wheel

pulley—a rope around a wheel with a grooved rim; a pulley makes it easier to lift or move objects

Internet SITES

FactHound offers a safe, fun way to find Internet sites related to this book. All of the sites on FactHound have been researched by our staff.

Here's all you do:

Visit *www.facthound.com*

Type in this code: 9781429682589

Glosario

el cable—un alambre grueso

el eje—una barra en el centro de una rueda alrededor de la cual gira la rueda

el engranaje—un rueda dentada que encaja en otra rueda dentada

la grúa—una máquina con un brazo largo usado para levantar y mover objetos pesados

la polea—una cuerda alrededor de una rueda con una hendidura; una polea facilita levantar o mover objetos

Sitios DE INTERNET

FactHound brinda una forma segura y divertida de encontrar sitios de Internet relacionados con este libro. Todos los sitios en FactHound han sido investigados por nuestro personal.

Esto es todo lo que tienes que hacer:

Visita *www.facthound.com*

Ingresa este código: 9781429682589

 **¡Algo súper divertido!** Hay proyectos, juegos y mucho más en **www.capstonekids.com**

31

Index

axles, 12, 13, 14,
  16, 17
bicycles, 24, 25
cables, 19
cranes, 19
gears, 20, 22, 24, 25,
  27, 28, 29
motors, 22

paddle wheels, 29
pulleys, 18, 19
robots, 22
sizes, 4
teeth, 20, 24
watches, 27

Índice

bicicletas, 24, 25
cables, 19
dientes, 20, 24
ejes, 12, 13, 14, 16, 17
engranajes, 20, 22, 24,
  25, 27, 28, 29
grúas, 19

motores, 22
poleas, 18, 19
relojes de pulsera, 27
robots, 22
ruedas de paleta, 29
tamaños, 4

32

A+ Books are published by Capstone Press,
1710 Roe Crest Drive, North Mankato, Minnesota 56003.
www.capstonepub.com

 Books published by Capstone Press are manufactured with paper
containing at least 10 percent post-consumer waste.

Library of Congress Cataloging-in-Publication Data
Weakland, Mark.
  [Gears go, wheels roll. Spanish & English]
  Los engranajes trabajan, las ruedas ruedan = Gears go, wheels roll / por/by
Mark Weakland.
     p. cm.—(Comienza la ciencia = Science starts)
  Includes index.
  Summary: "Simple text and photographs explain the basic science behind
wheels and gears—in both English and Spanish"—Provided by publisher.
  ISBN 978-1-4296-8258-9 (library binding)
  1. Gearing—Juvenile literature.2. Wheels—Juvenile literature. I. Title. II. Title:
Gears go, wheels roll. III. Series.
TJ181.5.W4318 2012
621.8'33—dc23   2011028672

Credits
Jenny Marks, editor; Strictly Spanish, translation services; Alison Thiele,
designer; Eric Manske, bilingual book designer; Marcie Spence, media
researcher; Laura Manthe, production specialist

Photo Credits
Capstone Studio: Karon Dubke, cover; iStockphoto: silverlining56, 14–15,
ssj414, 8–9, Ugurbarskan, 19; Shutterstock: afaizal, 11, Alexander V Evstafyev,
20–21, Anyka, 26–27, Christian Lagerek, 5, DeshaCAM, 6–7, Galina Barskaya,
4, GWImages, 1, Jamie Robinson, 12–13, jordache, 2–3, Maridav, 24–25,
Mikael Damkier, 16–17, pandapaw, 18, Steve Mann, 28–29, Supertrooper, 10,
Theodore Littleton, 22–23.

Note to Parents, Teachers, and Librarians
The Comienza la ciencia/Science Starts series supports national education
standards related to science. This book describes and illustrates gears and
wheels in both English and Spanish. The images support early readers in
understanding the text. The repetition of words and phrases helps early
readers learn new words. This book also introduces early readers to subject-
specific vocabulary words, which are defined in the Glossary section. Early
readers may need assistance to read some words and to use the Glossary,
Internet Sites, and Index sections of the book.

Printed in the United States of America in North Mankato, Minnesota.
102012   006949R